Python Crash Course

*A Complete Step-by-Step
Beginner Guide for
Python Coding,
NumPy, Pandas,
and Data
Visualization*

Table of Contents

Introduction

Who is meant to read this book?

This book Python Crash Course: *A Complete Step-by-Step Beginner Guide for Python Coding, NumPy, Pandas, and Data Visualization* is meant for any individual who is interested in Python programming. The experts who want to learn more. For beginners who want to learn everything and other professionals like finance and economy experts. Several individuals would like to earn from Python programming. You will learn all that from the book.

What will you learn from this book?

This book will clearly elaborate on the definition of Python programming, how you can use it, and the people who can benefit from it. There is enough information on what you can do with the information. You will get all the information you need on how important Python programming is to economists and in your workplace. Do you know that you can earn money from Python programming? If your answer is no, do not worry; all the information you need is clearly illustrated.

There are different concepts when it comes to Python programming, on the terms used, how to install Python, the courses offered, and what job you can get with Python skills. There are different operating systems that are used for Python programming like Linux, Windows, and OS X and how you can do troubleshooting. There are different variables and data types like classes, functions, and dictionaries. Data visualization and web applications are chapters that are important to learn and understand. You need to know what the list is, how to change, remove, add elements on the list, and you will know how to organize a list.

Chapter 1: Python Programming

What is Python Programming?

This is a programming language that is objected-oriented and of high level and uses semantics. It is a high level in terms of structures in data and a combination of dynamic typing and binding. This is what makes it attractive to be used for Rapid Application Development and for connecting different elements.

Python with its simplicity and learning with ease helps in reading the programming language, and that is why it reduces the cost to maintain the program. Python encourages the program modularity and code reuse; this is because it supports different packages and modules. The standard library and the Python interpreter can be found in binary form. It is not necessary to charge all the available platforms and can be distributed freely.

Most programmers love the Python program because they offer great productivity. The edit-test debug is a cycle that is fast and does not need any compilation process. It is easier to debug a Python program; it will not cause any segmentation fault. An exception is raised when an error is discovered by the interpreter. When the exception is not known by the program, the interpreter prints a trace. The debugger, on a level of sourcing, will allow being inspecting any variables. There will be a settling of breakpoints, arbitrary expressions, and stepping on the code at any time. The Python is what writes the debugger, the easier, and a quick debugging method and programs of adding prints on the source and statements.

Python is open-source; this means you can use them freely for any commercial applications. Python is programmed to work on UNIX, Windows, and Mac and can be transferred to Java. Python is a language that helps in scripting and helps in web applications for different content.

It is like Perl and Ruby. Python is helped by several imaging programs; users are able to create customized extensions. There are different web applications supporting Python API like Blender and GIMP.

This information given on Python programming is beneficial for both the newbies and the experienced ones. Most of the experienced programmers can easily learn and use Python. There is an easier way to install Python. Most distributors of UNIX and Linux have the recent

Python. That is the reason why most computers come already installed with Python. Before you start using Python, you need to know which IDEs and text editors' best work with Python. To get more help and information, you can peruse through introductory books and code samples.

The Python idea was discovered in 1980 after the ABC language. Python 2.0 was introduced, it had features like garbage collection and list comprehensions; which are used in reference cycle collection. When Python 3.0 was released in 2008, it brought about a complete language revision. Python is primarily used for developing software and webs, for mathematics and scripting systems. The latest version of Python is known a Python 3 while Python 2 is still popular. Python was developed to help in reading and similar aspects to different languages like English and emphasis on Mathematics.

A new line is used to complete a Python command, as opposed to other programming languages that normally use semi-colons. It depends on indentation, whitespace, and defining the scope.

How to use Python Programming

Before using Python, you first need to install and run it on your computer, and once you do that, you will be able to write your first program. Python is known as a programming platform that cuts across multiple platforms. You can use it on Linux, macOS, Windows, Java, and .NET machines freely and as an open-source. Most of the Linux and Mac machines come preinstalled even though on an outdated version. That is the main reason why you will need to install the latest and current version.

An easier way to run Python is by using Thonny IDE; this is because it is bundled with the latest version of Python. This is an advantage since you will not need to install it separately. To achieve all that, you can follow the simple steps below:

✓ First, you will need to download Thonny IDE

✓ Then run the installer in order to install it on your computer

✓ Click on File option, then new. Save the file on .py extension, for instance, morning.py or file.py. You are allowed to use any name for the file, as long as it ends with .py. Write the Python code on the file before saving it.

✓ To run the file, click on RUN, the run current script. Alternatively, click on F5 in order to run it.

There is also an alternative to install Python separately; it does not involve installing and running Python on the computer. You will need to follow the listed steps below:

- ✓ Look for the latest version of Python and download it.

- ✓ The next step is to run the installer file in order to install Python

- ✓ When installing, look for Add Python to environment variables. This will ensure that Python is added to the environment variables and that will enable you to run Python from any computer destination and part. You have the advantage to choose the path to install Python.

- ✓ When you complete the process of installing, you can now run Python.

There is also an alternative and immediate mode to run Python. When Python is installed, you will type Python on the command line; the interpreter will be in immediate mode. You can type Python code, and when you press enter, you will get the output. For instance, when you type 1 + 1 and then press enter, you will get the output as 2. You can use it as a calculator, and you quit the process, type quit, then press enter.

The second way to do it is by running Python on the Integrated Development Environment. You can use any editing software in order to write the Python script file. All you need to do is to save it the extension .py, and it is considered a lot easier when you use an IDE. The IDE is a feature that has distinctive and useful features like file explorers, code hinting, and syntax checking and highlighting that a programmer can use for application development.

You need to remember that when you install Python, there is an IDE labeled IDLE that will also be installed. That is what you will use to run Python on the computer and it is considered the best IDE for beginners. You will have an interactive Shell when IDLE is opened. This is the point where you can have a new file and ensure that you save it as a .py extension.

Who can use Python Programming?

There is a big challenge out there in choosing a programming language that you can use for your coding businesses. The bigger question is which language are you supposed to learn? Python is a program that is easy to use, and there are known companies that use it. This is one of the reasons why you should adapt to its uses. This is also the reason why worldwide developers have taken advantage.

- **Google**: Since the beginning of Python, Google has been its supporter. They choose Python because it was easy to maintain it, deploy, and faster in delivery.

The first web-crawling spider used for Google was in Java 1.0. It was difficult to use and maintain, and they had to do it again on Python. Python is one of the main programming languages that Google uses, the others include Java, C++, and Go that are used for production. Python is an important part of Google. They have been using it for many years, and it remains a system that is evolving and grows. Many engineers that work for Google prefer using Python. They keep seeking engineers with Python skills.

- **Facebook**: Production engineers that work for Facebook have a positive comment about Python. This has made Python among the top three programming languages after C++ and Hack. Facebook adopted Python because it is easy to use. With over 5000 services on Facebook, this is definitely the best programming language. The engineers do not need to maintain or write much coding, and this allows them to focus on live improvements. This is one of the reasons why Facebook infrastructure scales efficiently. Python is used for infrastructure management, for network switch setup, and for imaging.

- **Instagram**: From 2016, engineers working for Instagram declared that they were running the biggest Django web framework that was entirely written in Python. The engineers stated that they like Python because of the simple way to use it and how practical it is. That is why the engineers have invested their resources and time in using Python in all their trades. In recent times, Instagram has moved their codes from Python 2.7 to Python 3.

- **Spotify**: Spotify is a music-streaming platform that uses Python as its programing language for back end services and data analysis. The reason why Spotify decided to use Python is that they like the way it works in writing and in coding. Spotify will use its analytics in order to offer its users recommendations and suggestions. For the interpretation, Spotify uses Luigi that collaborates with Hadoop. The source will handle the libraries that work together. It will consolidate all the error logs and helps in troubleshooting and redeployment.

- **Quora**: Before implementing their idea, Quora decided to use Python programming for their question and answer platform. The Quora founders decided to go for Python because it was easy to read and write it. For great performance, they implemented C++.

Python is still considered because of the frameworks it has like Pylons and Django.

- **Netflix**: Netflix uses Python programming language to help in data analysis from their servers. They also use that in coding and other Python applications. It uses Python in the Central Alert Gateway and tracking any security history and changes.
- **Dropbox**: This cloud storage system uses Python for the desktop client. Their programs are coded in Python. They use different libraries for Windows and Mac. And the reason being it is not preinstalled on any Mac or Windows and the Python version differs.
- **Reddit**: Python programming language was used to implement Reddit. They choose Python because it has different versions of code libraries, and it was flexible to develop it.

What can you do with Python Programming?

There are numerous applications for Python programming, like machine learning, data science, and web development. In addition, other several projects can use Python skills:

- With Python programming, you are able to automate boring stuff; this is the best approach for beginners. It helps with spreadsheet updates and renaming files. When you get to master Python basics, then this is the best point to start with. With the information, you will be able to create dictionaries, web scraping, creating objects, and working on files.

- Python will help you stay on top of the prices that are set on Bitcoin. Bitcoin and cryptocurrency have become a popular investment; this is because of its price fluctuation. In order to know the right move in regards to Bitcoin, you will need to be alert on their prices. With Python, it is possible to create a price notification for Bitcoin. This is the best way to start on crypto and Python.

- When your intention and plan is to create a calculator, the Python is the best programming language. You will be able to build back-end and front-end services, which are the best when it comes to deployment. It is important to create applications that users can easily use. If your interest is in UX and UI design, then Python has a graphical user interface that is easy to work with.

- Python is the best programming language to use when mining data from Twitter. With the influx of technology and the internet, it is easy to get data and information easily. Data analytics is a very important concept; it involves what people are talking about and their behavioral patterns. To get all the answers, Twitter is the best place to start with when your interest is in data analysis. There is a data-mining project on Twitter, and that is when your Python skills will come handy.

- You will have the ability to create a Microblog with a flask. In recent times, most people have a blog. But again, it is not a bad idea to have your personal hub online. With Instagram and Twitter, microblogging has become a popular concept. With Python skills, you will be able to create your own microblog. When you are into web development, you do not need to be worried about knowing Flask. You can learn about it online and then move to Django which helps in web applications on a large scale.

- With Python skills, it is possible to build a Blockchain. The main reason for the development of blockchain was financial technology, even though it is spreading to other industries. As of now, blockchains can be used for any type of transaction, like medical records or real estate. When you get to build one for yourself, you will understand it better. You need to remember that, blockchain is not just for the individuals who are interested in crypto. When you build one, you will have a creative way for technology implementation to your own interest.

- You can bottle your Twitter feed with your Python skills, and this will help in web applications. You can create a simple web app that can help in navigation on your Twitter feed. You will not be using Flask, but rather Bottle; a low-dependency approach that is easy and quick to implement.

- There are PyGames that are easy to play with Python skills. You can use the skills to code several games and puzzles. With the Pygame library, it is easier to create your own games and developing it. It is an open and free source with computer graphics and sound libraries, and it helps in adding up interactive functions in the application. There are different games that can be used for library creation.

- With Python, it is possible to create something in relation to storytelling. Since the language is easy to use, that is

why it creates a better environment
for development and interaction.

Importance of Python Programming in the Economics

Most people ask if it is important for economists to learn any programming language. The answer is that it is important since they will use the skills to test and crush data sets. Most of the economist use Python as their main programming language to help with efficiency in order to run complex models. The idea of data analysis is used by other professionals not only by data scientists. Economists learn how to code in order to enjoy the ability to handle bigger data software. Large data can now be handled in spreadsheets when you use the new systems and all that can be done in a shorter time. That is the main reason why economists are adapting to the Python programming language.

Big data is what is used by different people all over. It helps in coding and for market and business intelligence. More spectrums of solutions are created by tech individuals, and they are not just for data scientists. This is why many economists are using and learning programming languages. Economists have been adapting to Python at a slower rate since they did not mostly depend on the data as compared to data scientists. They have adapted to the programming languages because of its flexibility, the breadth of functionalities, development, speed in computing, and the ability to operate between different systems.

Economists will deal with data that is on both low and high frequency. This is because of the increase in digitization and computing. The modern economy brings about greater power in computing and data sources. Years back, coding was used for only back office works, unlike recent times when it is used for front functions, and that is the reason why the use of Python has increased.

Importance of Python Programming at the Workplace

Several benefits come with learning Python if you have not learned the language. There is no need to panic because Python is a program that is easy to learn and can be used to learn other programming languages. You will understand the importance of Python since it is adopted by different companies like Instagram, Disney, Nokia, IBM, Pinterest, and Google. When you learn about Python, you will have the skills needed to succeed and make good money at it.

- Python programming language helps in developing prototypes, and the reason is that it is quick to learn and work with.
- Most of the data mining and automation rely on Python. The reason being that language is better for general tasks.
- With Python, you will get a better and productive environment for coding, unlike what most programming languages like Java and C++ will do. Most coders claim that with Python, they are better organized and productive when it comes to their work.
- Since Python is not complicated and any beginner can easily read, learn, and understand, this means that anyone can work with the programming language. All that you will need is patience and practice to excel with the language. Python helps most programmers and development in large-scale dimensions.
- Django is an open-source used in web development and application that is powered by Python. With Python, it is easier in improving the maintenance and readability of codes. Python helps in securing coding with updates and maintenance. The reason being it helps in developing quality in the software application. You will also be able to

demonstrate all the concepts when using syntax rules. The quality that Python offers in terms of maintenance and readability makes it the best programming language. You can even use English keywords instead of punctuations.

- Python helps with multiple paradigms that help a programmer know what is relevant in the work environment and requirement. Since Python supports different paradigms in programming, it is capable to feature different concepts that relate to functional programming. With Python, it is possible to develop a software application that is complicated and large.

- Python help in integrating with different operating systems and interpreting different codes. There is a possibility to redevelop this application without recompiling.

- Python is able to provide better results as compared to the other programming language because of its library that is robust and big. From the library, it is possible to select the best as per the requirements and add more functionality to that. The feature will prevent having any additional code writing.

- Python helps in simplifying any complicated software. This programming language helps in data analytics and visualization in any program that is developing. When you are familiar with Python, you get to complete complex solutions without putting in a lot of time.

How can you earn using Python Programming?

- **Blogging**: Python programming helps in creating a blog, and the blog is used in making money. There are different types of blogging. You can specialize in programming as your niche in blogging. There are numerous ways to use your blog as a programmer. This includes online coding, charging your premium content, and affiliate links. Ensure all your content is SEO friendly with the relevant keywords that are what is used in ranking your page. In addition, SEO optimization should be on both on and off-page. You will be guaranteed of traffic to the site.
- **Apps Development**: Your programming skills will be beneficial when you develop an app and monetize it. This programming helps in attaining that.

Ensure that you market your app, and use the automatic coding apps that will help in creating the app in a few minutes. With a great marketing technique, you will be able to make money out of app development. In order to sell it, you need to launch it on the App store.

- **Freelancing**: This is a situation whereby you offer your services online. You should ensure that you look for the available online platforms and what works for you. You will be able to work from your own work schedule and make money while doing that. Some of the genuine and known platforms include Guru, Freelancer, and Upwork. You can also pitch directly to clients and offer your programming services.

- You can earn using your Python skills when you make a plugin. The other alternative is having a theme on Wordpress. The best way to do it is by developing many apps and smaller modules like themes and WordPress plugins. This is a great way to make money coding online. Most websites use Wordpress, so if you can create WordPress plugins, you are assured of making a lot of money.

- Another way is to be an online educator and start selling your online courses. All this is possible when you use your Python skills and do coding. Most people are adopting online courses where people who cannot attend classes can still learn. When you have a personal website, you can offer free courses and tutorials and have traffic. You can teach many students in economics and finance on how to code and Python skills.

- When you join coding competitions, you will be using your Python skills and still earn some good money. You can do development, data science, and design. When you are a winner, you are paid and get access to big companies who are on the lookout for competent coders.

- Your Python skills will help in website creation. You can share your programming tips and then display what you have. Ensure that your website shows all your skills, your bans, and your portfolio as a coder. When you have your brand established, you will get more clients that will be willing to get your services and consultation, and you can charge for that. A website can bring your earnings through Google Adsense, affiliate marketing, and sponsored ads.

Chapter 2: Python Programming Concepts

Basic Concepts in Python Programming

The first step to learning Python programming is to make sure that you have understood the ways of learning the language. By understanding how to learn is the most critical skills needed in computer programming. The importance of knowing how to learn is that languages evolve, new libraries are created, and tools upgraded. You must be able to keep up with the changes to be successful in the programming world.

In the modern world, one of the most used languages is Python. This is not just a language, and it is a method of how to do things in a simple and the right way. It is a common high-level language used in open-source. Python is a vast language, and the more you learn about Python, the more information you will need to learn. This is an ironic statement, but that's how it is. Python uses a simple object-oriented approach and high-level data structures. Pythons also use simple dynamic typing and syntax.

Python is a language that is compact, fast, and can efficiently work in any operating system. In addition, if research, you will notice that most of the sites run on Python such as YouTube and Google. Pyramid and Django are frameworks that support Python exclusively, same as the micro-framework like Flask and Bottle, which also supports Python.

Python programming is mostly made up of English language keywords. You will master Python if you can learn the keywords. It will need some practice, and you need to familiarize yourself with the basic concepts before you begin. So, let's start by going through some of them:

- Properties

Python is dynamically typed, and there is no need to state the variables. The variable is case sensitive; the types are enforced. For example, VAR and var are identified as two separate variables. To find out how any of the objects work, type the following command:

help(object)

Also, dir(object) to find all the methods of a certain option and use object.__doc__ to know the document string.

- Data types

The next concept is data types. Lists, dictionaries, and tuples are data structures in Python. There are sets of libraries that are available in all versions of Python. Lists are the same as the one-dimensional array, and there can be lists of other different lists. The associative arrays, such as Dictionaries, while the one-dimensional arrays are the Tuples. Python arrays are any type, and its always zero. A negative number starts from the end to the beginning.

- Functions

The keyword 'def' is used to declare functions. Mandatory and optional arguments are simultaneously set in the function through assigning default values. An argument is assigned a value, and the functions can be returned to the tuple, which can effectively return values using the tuple unpacking. Connecting an object to a variable will remove an older one and also replace the immutable type.

There is a lot of information on Python programming. As always, the main aim is to learn to program, mostly Python. Keep on experimenting and practicing programming to gain the skills and experience. It has a massive array of libraries and functions that you learn and taps into. There are great books and online resources to learn in-depth about Python programming, from error handling, subsets, and classes. You will encounter syntax errors galore, however, keep moving ahead, and you can join the fantastic Python communities and various resources, and you will master it in no time.

The Terms used in Python Programming

As it is the case for any skill, before going full-fledged into practicing the mode, it's important to learn the basic terms that are used in that domain. To better understand your domain, you should learn the terms. For a beginner in Python Programming, we bring a few essential terms that you can be your learning 101 guides.

Below goes the programming terminology for beginners:

- Algorithm

A set of rules that are created to solve an exact error. Tan error can be complex, such as converting video files to a different format or simply such as adding two numbers.

- Program

This is an organized collection of instructions that performs a specific function when executed. It is processed by the CPU, an acronym for the central processing unit of the computer, before executed. Microsoft Word is an example of a program that enables users to create and edit documents. Also, the browsers used are programs that are created to help users to browse the internet.

- API

API is an acronym for Application Programming Interfaces. Sets of rules and procedures of building software applications. The APIs help with communication with third party programs, which is used to build different software. Major companies like Facebook and Twitter frequently use APIs to assist the developers to easily gain access to their services.

- Bytecode

Python combines the source code into bytecode, an internal presentation of the Python program in a CPython interpreter. Basically, the bytecode is an intermediate language running a virtual machine. The virtual machine is converted into machine code for it to execute it; however, the one-byte can not run on a different virtual machine.

- Bug

A bud is a term used to refer to an unexpected error in hardware or software, which causes it not to function. Bugs are often regarded as small computer glitches; however, bugs are life-threatening conditions and causing substantial financial losses. That's why it is important to focus on the process of finding bugs before programs in the applications, and this process is called testing.

- Code

This is a term used to describe a written set of rules that are written using protocols of different languages like Python or Java. And also an informal use of the code describing text that is written in a specific language, and the reference code can be made for different languages such as CCS Code or HTML Code.

- Command-line interface

This is a user interface that is based on the text, and it is used in viewing and managing computer files. The interface is also referred to as the command-line user, character user, and console users. In the early 60s, 70s, and 80s, the primary means of interaction with computers on terminals was the command-line interface.

- Compilation

Creating an executable program by writing the code in a compiled programming language is known as compilation. With compiling, the computer understands the program and runs it without using the programming software that was used to create it. The compiler translates the computer programs that were written using numbers and letters to a machine language program. C++ is an example of a compiler.

- Constants

This is also referred to as Const is a term that describes a value that doesn't change through the execution of the program as opposed to a variable. Constant is fixed and cannot be changed; it can be a string, number, or character.

- Data Types

This is a group of a particular type of data. A computer cannot differentiate between a name or a number as a human, so it uses a special internal code to know the difference in the types of data it receives and how to process it. There are various data types, which include character, which is the alphabets, the boolean values are the TRUE or FALSE, the integer is the numbers, and the floating-point number is the decimal numbers.

- Array

The array is a list of a grouped type of data values, and the values have the same data type; however, they are different by the positioning in the array. For example, the age of students in a class is an array because they are all numbers, and also, the student's names in a class are array because of its a character data type.

- Declaration

This is a statement describing a variable, function, or other identifiers. It helps the compiler to identify the word, understand its meaning, and how to continue the process. They are essential, however, optional and are useful depending on the type of programming language.

- Exception

The unexpected and special condition that is encountered during the execution of a program. This is also an error or a condition that changes the program to a different path. For example, when a program loads a file from the disk but the file does not exist. In order to avoid any fatal error, the highly important to handle and eradicate the exceptions in the program code.

- Coroutine

A subroutine enters one point and exits in another point while a coroutine is generalized meaning; it enters, exits, and also resumes at many different points. A coroutine is implemented with the async def statement.

- Generic Function

Multiple functions are implementing a similar operation for different types. A dispatch algorithm will decide on which implementation to be used during a call.

- Python Expression

A piece of code that is evaluated to a value. It's a collection of expression elements such as function calls, names, operators, and literals. An if-statement is not an assignment or an expression because it doesn't return a value.

- Python Decorator

A function that returning another function. It joins functionality without modifying it.

- Loop

It is a series of instructions repeating a similar process that continues until a condition is completed, and it receives a command to stop. Then a question is asked on the program, and an answer will command the program to act, and then the loop continues to achieve a similar task. The process continues until there is no required action, and the code proceeds on. Loops are one of the most straightforward and powerful concepts in programming.

How to start Python Programming for Data Analysis

- Learn Python Fundamentals

We all start from somewhere. The first step is learning the Python programming basics then learn an introduction to data analysis. One of the essential tools to use to start early in your journey is Jupyter Notebook, which is packaged with Python libraries to assist you in learning both Python programming and data analysis.

- Practice Mini Python Projects

With hands-on learning, you will be surprised how soon you will be ready to take on small Python projects. For example, tying things likes calculators for an online game or trying a program that gathers the weather from Google in a particular city. By doing mini projects like these will enable you to learn Python. Such programming projects are the standard for all languages and the perfect way to better understand the basics. Start by building your experience with APIs and begin web scraping. Python will help you learn to program while learning web scarping will assist you in gathering data.

- Learn Python Data Science Libraries

Unlike other programming languages, in Python, there is the best way to do something. The best and essential Python libraries for data analysis are Matplotlib, Pandas, and Numpy. For data visualization, use the Matplotlib library. For exploring and playing with data, Pandas and Numpy are the best library to use.

- Build a Data Science Portfolio as you Learn Python

Building a portfolio is essential for an aspiring data analysis. The projects should be various datasets, and the portfolio doesn't need to have a specific theme. Find a dataset that you have interest in and find a plan of putting all of them together. Displaying such projects help with future employers, and it shows that you took the time to learn Python and other essential programming skills.

- Apply Advanced-Data Analysis Techniques

Focus on sharpening your skills, and your data analysis journey will be full of constant learning; however, there are advanced courses to help you cover all the bases. And be comfortable with classification and regression. Also, step into machine learning and using scikit-learn to create neural networks. In addition, programming projects involves creating models using live data feeds.

How to Install Python

Python is a common programming language for application development. Python design focuses on code readability and clear programming for both small and big projects. You are able to run modules and full application from a massive library of resources on the server. Python works on various operating systems, such as Windows. Installing Python on the Windows server is a straightforward process of downloading the installer, and running it on your server and configuring some adjustments can Python easier.

To begin working with Python, you will first need permission from the Python interpreter. There are different ways of achieving these:

✓ Python is available from the website Python.org. Download the right installer for your operating system and run it on the computer.

✓ Linux provides a packaging manager that you can use to run your install Python.

✓ The macOS uses a package manager called Homebrew to install Python.

✓ iOS and Android are mobile operating systems, and you will need to install apps that will support Python programming. And this is the best way to practice your coding skills at any time.

And the other way is by finding websites that provide the users the opportunity to get into Python interpreter online, and there is no need to install it on their computer. And also a chance that the Python will be preinstalled in your operating system. If that's the case, then the version might be outdated, and you need to get the latest version.

In this chapter, you will learn the process of setting up the Python on macOS, iOS, Windows, and Linux. Let's begin!

- Windows

Python does not come preinstalled in the Windows systems. However, installing Python is a straightforward process. All you need to do is to download Python installer on the website, Python.org, and then run the program.

Here is how you install it on Windows:

➣ **Downloading Python installer**
Opening your browser, get into the Python.org website, and move to the download page for Windows.
➣ Click on the heading "Python release for Windows and click on the link.

➤ Scroll down and select Windows 64-bit or 32-bit Windows.

When using Windows, you either download a 64 or a 32-bit. The difference between these two is,

➤ Use a 32-bit installer if you have a 32-bit processor.

➤ If you have a 64-bit system, then both of the versions will work on both of the purposes. Using a 32-bit will require less memory; however, using a 64-bit will work best with applications of intensive computation.

➤ When you are not sure of which version to install, choose a 64-bit version.

Additionally, when you install the incorrect version, and you wish to change it and choose another version, you may do that by uninstalling Python and re-installing it by getting the version from Python.org.

• Running the installer

When you chose and downloaded the installer, then double-click the downloaded file and run it. You will see a dialog box that has a prompting button instructing you to run the installation. Don't forget to click the box that indicates "Adding Python to PATH"; this will confirm that the interpreter is added in the execution path. The final step is to click 'Install now,' and this is all the required steps. After a few moments, a working Python will be installed on the system.

- Windows Subsystem for Linux

When your computer has Windows 10 Creators installed, you have a different way of installing Python. A feature called Windows Subsystem for Linux is used in this version, and you can run the Linux environment straight into Windows without having to use the virtual machine. After you have installed the type of Linux distribution you require, go ahead and install Python from the console window. A similar way can be done if you are natively using a Linux distribution.

- Linux

Most Linux distribution comes with preinstalled Python; however, it might not be the latest version. To be able to know what version you have, there is a process you can do to find out. Open a prompt window and then try the following commands below:

Python version.

Python2 version.

Python3 version.

The version of the commands from the three commands will answer with the version. If it is not the latest version, you will install the newest version. The procedure of this depends on the Linux distribution running on your computer. It's much useful to use Pyenv, a tool used for multiple Python version management on Linux.

- Ubuntu

There are different versions of the Ubuntu distribution, and the installations are different. Identify your Ubuntu versions by trying these commands:

$lsb release a

No-LSB module available

Distributors ID: Ubuntu

Descriptions: Ubuntu-16.04.4.

Release-16.04.

Code name-xenial.

Ubuntu versions 16.10 and 17.04 don't have the Python 3.6, as it's the universal repository.

- Linux Mint

Both Ubuntu and Mint use similar packaging management systems, making life much easier. Installation instruction for Ubuntu can also be used in Mint. A deadsnakes PPA working well with Mint.

- Debian

Some evidence shows Ubuntu's 16.10 method can also work for Debian, however, there is no path for it to work on Debian 9. But you can make Python from the following source.

One disadvantage of Debian is, it doesn't install Sudo commands by default. Before installing Debian, you are required to check a compiled source from the Python instruction:

$-su.

$apt-get-install sudo

$-vi /etc/sudo

Then use sudo vim commands or any preferred text editor to open /etc/sudoers file. Adding the following text line at the end and changing "your_username" with the real usernames:

your_usernameALL=(ALL)ALL

- Open SUSE

There are various websites which outline ways of getting zypper to add the newest Python; however, they might be outdated. They don't successfully work, and it's best to build Python from the source. Begin by installing the development tool that is completed in YaST through the menu or the zypper.

$sudu zypper install-tpatterndevel_C_C++

The procedure will take some time, and it involves installing 154 packages; however, when completed, you will be able to build the source.

- Arch Linux

It's fairly strict to keep up with the Python release. Arch Linux might be preinstalled, and if it is, it is not the newest version, use the following command:

$packman -S Python

Chapter 3: Python Programming Lessons

How to Learn about Python Programming

The first thing you should know before learning Python is that this is not going to be easy. This should not scare you at all because I think there is a really good way to make all these a little friendlier. Many beginner tutorial videos talk of how Python programming language gets complicated with time and how the long run is not going to be so much exciting. Well, it really depends on what really fascinates you into the Python world.

Let us venture into some of the features and thoughts that an individual is highly expected to dive into in the first place.

✓ Think of what dived you into considering Python language.

It is super easy and fun to learn something if there is a grand reason behind all that. Frankly, Python language learning needs massive motivation so as to grasp every good detail, and therefore, your objective of learning should be your motivation so as to eventually evade boredom. Pick a field area that you are interested in and one that you are so ready to put your massive efforts into. Multiple kinds of fields are available, for instance, games, mobile development, websites, and many more that actually call for good knowledge and skills in Python programming language. Getting motivated to acquire all these so as to specialize in your desired field area should definitely be the main key to learning and getting advanced in the Python language world. You sure got this.

✓ Master the basic syntax.

Apparently, the basic syntax is the most important factor in your Python world foundation. Concentrate deep on the basic syntax and get to master how the structure behaves and the various operations involved. However, it is advisable that you do not really need to spend much time in this because you actually get to master the basic syntax as you try to implement them in the various projects that you may consider to start with. This will also provide an opportunity for the novice to learn from the possible mistakes that are likely to be committed when coding with Python language.

✓ Involving multiple structural works.
Learning and implementing out the new things learned has always been the best way of learning in history. Well, get the basic part of the Python language basics and try to implement the concept learned in various projects that use Python language. As discussed, this will help the learner to identify the faults that are likely to be committed during programming, learn from every error and get really advanced in working with Python projects and coming up with viable projects that are pretty good in solving human problems.

✓ Build something.
Structural work will definitely get you into great curiosity and fascinated by what you can actually build and

get it to be productive. This is definitely a good strategy that will get you into a bigger position in the Python world. What is more amazing is that you will not be implementing what has been learned but also get to grasp so many new concepts and ideas as you get along in your learning journey. Always try to commit to some various projects by yourself and get to know how far you can go and also where to rectify in your learning journey so as to become an amazing expert in the Python programming world.

Start with the basic kind of projects as you try to get advanced with time where you will be dealing with the tough kind ones that you be amazed at how simpler they may sometimes get a thing that you totally did not expect.

✓

Collaborative measures.
It is highly recommended that, as a learner, you ought to surround yourself with peers who are also learning the same language as you. Well, two heads are actually better than one, and every individual

normally has different views and angles that he or she comprehends a certain concept. Go and exchange ideas and work on multiple projects once in a while and see how far you can go as a team and see the scope of new things and new ideas that you are capable of grasping. Learning as a community creates that positive attitude and the willingness and passion to learn more gets to increase with time.

✓ Open-source.

Fortunately, many companies normally publish various open sources on the internet of multiple software that they are working on. This should give the learner the opportunity to get involved in certain pull requests, an activity that will developers get to view your code and see what you have been working on. This may even land you your first job at any of the desired software companies and eventually get to grow as a person. Furthermore, contributing to various source codes on the internet will also enhance your communication with multiple developers around the world, and you eventually get to grow in your career and also as a person.

✓ Make coding a habit.

Mastering and grasping the basics in Python programming language calls for good consistency and great motivation for success to follow your way. Spare around 30 minutes of your time every single day as you commence your learning journey and see coding becoming your habit, especially if you are totally new to the programming world. The start is always the hard part but I believe with the amount of full energy that one entails at the starting point will definitely pass you through the successful journey in this Python language world. All the best.

Where can you learn about Python Programming?

There exist multiple and several learning sources that an interested programmer can venture into and grasp the wide knowledge and skills of the Python programming language. For instance:

✓ **Websites**

- Cybrary

    The website entails various Python programming courses for beginners who have a huge interest in the Cybersecurity field. The courses are super helpful and get you started towards your end goal journey.

- Sololearn

    This is another amazing site full of several programming languages in wide knowledge, good structural examples, projects, challenges, and many other helpful tasks. Sololearn normally tutors from the basic steps to the complex and advanced steps with so many tips and assistance that will eventually get you through the end goal.

- Code academy

    Code academy is another online site that is contented with basic, intermediate, and advanced levels of various programming languages. A beginner can, therefore, expect to find practical and much detailed contents of Python programming language that will clearly create a huge impact in his or her technological world.

- **EDX**

    This is also a good learning site that just calls for signup and getting started with your new account where you will learn good Python learning skills and knowledge and eventually get the chance to acquire a certificate that is pretty much valid and one that will eventually get you to your first Python income-generating project.

- **GitHub**

    GitHub is common in most developers as a source of learning and getting advanced in various programming languages through the wide use of open sources. Developers are likely to get engaged in various pull requests and get to collaborate with various kinds of Python developers from all over the world on various viable projects. This will not only give the developers the opportunity to learn new concepts about Python language but also enhance appropriate communication between developers.

- Stack overflow

    Stack overflow is basically an online platform where developers get to inquire about anything, discuss a certain topic, get answers for their unknown questions in mind, and basically get to learn anything in which they highly desire to learn. A developer interested to grasp a certain complicated topic on Python language can inquire, and he or she will surely get much assistance.

- YouTube

    YouTube has become a famous type of social media that is pretty much used for learning purposes. This is because it is much practical and structural as depicted by its most online learning videos. Most companies like Edureka have their accounts on YouTube where people are obligated to subscribe so as to follow up on their learning videos and also be informed on the Python language day to day updates.

✓ Python books.

    Books are famous in learning because they are much detailed and easier for reference purposes when trying to master a new programming language. Python books are available in the local libraries around your vicinity, local book stores, and even online via the Amazon site. Some of the most loved Python books include:

- Headfirst Python by Paul Burry - This book is highly recommended to the novice who is pretty much interested in grasping the basics of the Python language. The book entails illustrations and so much great assistance that a beginner would call for when getting into the Python programming world.
- Python crash course by Eric Matthes – The book immerses an individual into several hands-on projects that he or she is expected to venture into as part of the learning journey. He or she is expected to learn the basic fundamentals of the Python programming language, and eventually becoming an accomplished beginner once the book is completed. Some of the fundamentals of the Python language entail popular Python web frameworks that are super important in web development.
- Python programming by John Zelle – The book is designed for the computer science students who have the intention of grasping the basic idea of Python programming

language for the purpose of their academic achievement.

✓

PDF and other texts.

The internet entails various kinds of PDFs that a learner can consider to opt-in and learn various concepts and the basic facts in Python programming. There exist various PDFs for the beginners and also the intermediate kind of learners where they are likely to get exposed to the good Python programming concepts and the basic facts and achieve the very best out of all these in the endpoint.

✓

Social media communities.

With the wide use of social media, it is so much easier for learners to learn together via various online sites like Whatsapp group, Telegram channels, Facebook communities, and so much more. Through these sites, developers are able to discuss the clear Python language concepts that appear to be much complicated to some people and even undertake various challenges together. Learning Python programming language through various tech communities has been confirmed to be so much helpful.

What is the Cost of Getting a Python Certification?

The cost of acquiring a Python certificate is getting gradually getting expensive with years. In recent times, acquiring a Python certificate at the moment can cost around 290$ to 350$ in most of the popular learning institutions like the Python institute. The amount of finances includes full examination fees that a programmer is required to go through before getting a valid Python certificate. Acquiring a Python certificate can land you to a brand new job if you are a new developer in the programming industry, and on the other hand, get you promoted to a much better position in your firm. I wish you all the best in Python studying and achieving your deserved certificate

The Best Python Course

As learners, we ought to commit ourselves to the best king of Python courses so as to grasp the best in all that, and eventually, come up with something really viable to the universe. Below are some of the best courses that a learner is pretty much expected to dive into and extract success from them:

✓

The numpy stack in Python
Identified as deep learning prerequisites course outline, this kind of course particularly targets programmers who are interested in data science and machine learning using the Python language. The programmer is likely to explore into several kinds of Python libraries, for instance, numpy, pandas, and scipy that will establish a perfect base for the programmer in deep machine learning, data science, and even artificial intelligence. The programmer is also likely to get exposed to the various advantages and the cons of utilizing certain Python libraries in their projects as they work on multiple data science and machine learning projects.

✓

Python core and advanced kind.
First, this course is totally free, and therefore, financial disabilities should definitely not be the reason as to why a particular programmer should not venture into this course. The course is much detailed

describing how Python should be installed, illustrating how a programmer is expected to execute his or her first program, Python command line, Python constructs, object-oriented programming with Python, Python libraries, Python libraries, and so much other Python basics that are super important.

✓

Python 3.0 boot camp for novice programmers.

If boot camp courses for Python programming language excites you, then this is the right side for you. Okay, I have good news; the course is totally free, and you are, therefore, not going to spend even a single dime from your savings. This is a simple, detailed, and particular kind of Python 3 programming course and the programmer is, in the end, expected to learn the basic concepts and working illustrations of the Python 3 programming language. The course is suitable for both those with no prior knowledge of Python programming and also advanced programmers.

✓ Learn Python programming in just 100 steps.

This is the perfect course for a programmer to learn the Python 3 basic steps and get a clear comprehension of what is actually is entailed. The course was founded a great and popular Udemy instructor and blogger from Udemy who outlines the basic Python programming concepts coupled up with the respective tools and integrated development environment that is constituted in the Python programming world. The programmer will also get the opportunity to venture into various hands-on exercises of different topics in Python like data structures, object-oriented programming, handling various kinds of Python errors, and in the end, get to work on various kinds of projects that will definitely turn out to be pretty much successful.

What Job can you get with Python?

Python language is widely used by large tonnes of companies in our current world. Some of the companies include Instagram, Reddit, Google, Spotify, Netflix, and even in our favorite local banks. Let us dive into some of the income-generating projects that are as a result of implementing Python language:

✓ A Python developer.

This career is best suited for a developer who is pretty much contented with Python language at a much wider scope, and he or she is well advanced with the programming language. A Python developer is involved in tasks like building and developing various websites, optimizing data algorithms, implementing various security measures and protecting data, solving multiple problems in data analytics, and also writing reusable and efficient kinds of codes. Well, being a developer exposes a developer to various income-generating tasks that can make eventually him or her land into good jobs in major startups in the world.

✓ Data Analysts

Most companies are looking for individuals with the ability to play with a large number of numbers using Python libraries like the scipy and pandas that are normally implemented in large data sets. An example of a company that is in great search of data analysts using Python is Bloomberg.

✓ A product manager.

A product manager basically talks to the users of a certain product directly and gets to grasp some important data from them concerning the product in question. Through this, they are able to derive new features for their products, spot the possible market gaps, improve on their current tools or acquire new tools for their products, and so much more. This is so exciting, right? Companies like Snapchat is hunting for such great individuals.

✓ Financial advisers.

Bank financial advisers are highly advanced in the Python programming language where they are able to master the behavior of people's bank accounts in form of several sets of data and various bank operations, hence provide guidance services to various customers who happen to be in need.

✓ Software engineering.

Software engineers are involved in analyzing the user's needs and designing, testing, and evaluating applications for the purpose of satisfying the users as part of the end goal. Software developers are happily paid large chunks of money, and they also get the opportunity to get exposed to greater career opportunities.

✓ Research analysts.

Research analysts are normally involved in researching, analyzing, and coming up with viable reports concerning a certain product in the market. They are able to succeed in this in-depth market research by implementing various Python libraries to the available sets of data of the products.

✓ Machine learning engineers.

Machine learning engineers normally develop multiple machines, software, and other computer systems that are highly capable of learning and implementing any kind of knowledge that has been comprehended and excluding the use of set instructions. This is what individuals advanced in a Python programming language can do with the kind of knowledge they have in their minds.

✓ Quality assurance engineer.

These kinds of engineers are able to track the development process of a product from the commencing point to the endpoint using various Python libraries and methods. Quality assurance engineers are super famous in the technology industry, and they are paid a good amount of money that is worth getting the right skills and knowledge using Python programming language and other various techniques.

✓ Web developer.

Python is a great part of website development through its various frameworks that offer a great part of website development. Some of the common frameworks of the

Python language include Django and the pyramid that are used by most website developers.

✓ Game developers.

With knowledge in Python libraries like the pygame and panda3D, a developer gets to acquire the skills and knowledge that is pretty much needed in developing various games. Game developers earn an average amount of salary that is still a goof financial figure.

Chapter 4: Operating Systems

What's your definition of an operating system? An operating system is a type of system software which allows users to run their application programs on their computing devices. Your computing devices ought to have an operating system that assists in the managing of your hardware resources and also provides services to your application programs. Python language, like any other programming language, also runs on various operating systems of your machines. The are various operating systems that support Python which include Linux, OS X, and also Windows. In this chapter, you shall learn on the various mentioned operating systems and also be aware of the different ways of Python troubleshooting.

Python on Linux

Linux is some sort of a Unix operating system that operates under the open-source license. An open-source operating system means that you can do some modification on the system software, and you can even distribute the modified version to others. Its ability to be performed some modification makes it so popular and preferred to, unlike the other operating systems. Linux operating system is supported by many devices such as mobile devices, computers and also servers.

How is this operating system used?

Almost all versions of this operating system provide user interfaces to users and manage their hardware resources. Moreover, web servers such as Apache utilize the Linux operating system as compared to other operating systems.

The different versions that exist for the Linux operating system are referred to as the distributions. These distributions can be downloaded online with no cost, saved on your USB drives, and installed on your preferred machines. The Linux distributions that exist include the following:

- ✓ Linux mint
- ✓ Debian
- ✓ Ubuntu
- ✓ Solus
- ✓ Fedora
- ✓ Opensuse
- ✓ Manjaro

Some of the Linux distributions are tailored for servers, desktops, and many other systems. The most commonly used Linux distributions for desktop are Ubuntu server and CentOS, which are free with no cost but do not offer support for their users. Contrarily, the distributions that offer support for their users but are costly include Red Hat distribution and SUSE Enterprise. This operating system is a secure and robust system, and hence there is no need for the users to install any antivirus software on their machines.

Which versions of Python can be run on Linux distributions?

Different versions of the Python language can be run on different Linux distributions. The most commonly used versions are Python version 2 and version 3. You are, however, mostly advised to use version 3 as compared to version 2, since it is actively maintained. The two versions have different syntax so you need to decide on only one version to use on your computing device.

How to use Python on your Linux distribution.

You can use Python on Linux using the Integrated Development Environment (IDLE). It is a graphical user interface that allows its users to write Python code on it. To use Python on your Linux distribution, you need to also install packages that are compatible with your distribution.

Some individuals prefer using the command line version to the IDLE versions. Ubuntu distribution normally comes with a command-line version already pre-installed which makes your work easier. You can decide to choose the version that you are comfortable with. Furthermore, most of the Ubuntu tools support Python as compared to other distributions.

At most times, a novice who uses a Linux operating system, normally run their first Python scripts on a command-line version before using Python text editors. With time, they get familiarized with the text editors and other programs known as interpreters. An interpreter is a program that converts the lines of codes written by a Python programmer in a way that a computer can easily understand. It enhances the programming, and the computers are able to process and execute the lines of code.

When using the command-line interface, right-click on your desktop and type in Python on the Linux terminal. Still, at the command prompt, you can type in "Hello world", and the text that is written will be displayed on the next line. This can be hectic sometimes, so many Python programmers decide to switch to using the Integrated Development Environment instead.

To get started with the IDLE on Linux operating system, you need to open a terminal window on your machine and type "idle", of course, without the quotes. After a while, a graphical shell will load. To be provided with some sort of text editor, click on the file, then click on a new window to begin writing a Python script. Try writing some lines of code on the text editor. Save your file with a .py extension and try running it by clicking on run then run a module from the menu. Above is all the information you need to know to get started with Python on a Linux operating system.

Python on OS X

You are lucky if you are an OS X user since most of your machines come when Python is already installed on them. For those who do not know if Python is installed on your machine, you can open a terminal and type Python –version. You should make plans for downloading a set up of Python if you do not have any from your machine. The few ways of installing Python on your OS X machine include the following:

✓ From the source
This method involves installing Python from the source code. Most programmers prefer this method with the desire of doing some customization on the binaries during the building process.

✓ From packaged binaries
You can get the Python binaries from the Python website which assists you in

making upgrades on your Python versions. You need to make sure that the Python version you want to download matches the type of your CPU architecture. The types are either 32 bits or 64 bits.

✓ Homebrew
This is the package manager for OS X. It enables its users to install, uninstall, and even make updates on their packages using the command line. It works the same as the **apt-get** that is available on Ubuntu distribution on Linux machines. It makes work easier for OS X users.

You need to install the latest Python version with the new features.

All Python programmers need a powerful development tool known as a text editor that assists them in their code execution and testing of their lines of code. Different Python programmers have different tastes of text editors. The default Python text editor for this operating system is the TextEdit which unfortunately does not support all the formatting options. You need to select another text editor great for you. There are, however, few Python text editors for the OS X operating system. Below is a list of the most preferred text editors to use on your OS X machine:

✓ IDLE.

This is the common and the simplest text editor most individuals use to get started with Python. It comes bundled together with Python set up during installation, and it's located in the application folder. It enables its users to perform modifications on their lines of code and also get to see the code results.

Let us now get started on how to launch IDLE on your OS X since most novice Python programmers use this text editor when beginning off with Python.

- Type in and click on the terminal on the search button located at the top right of your screen.
- A blank terminal window will load after a while.
- Type in "idle" on the terminal, and of course, without the quotes. Then press return.
- IDLE will start up definitely then get started with your Python programming.

Since this text editor does not have advanced features as compared to the other text editors, you can choose another text editor when you get familiarized with Python coding after some while.

✓ PyCharm.

This is the most popular Python text editor on an OS X operating system. It offers both the free and paid versions to its users. PyCharm was developed by Czech company Jetbrains back on 3rd February 2010. It makes work easier for its users by providing the necessary tools for analyzing their lines of code, debug on them, and also test on them. Most web developers use PyCharm when working with Django which is a Python open-source framework.

The three editions for PyCharm include the following:

- PyCharm Edu.
  PyCharm Edu is a free edition that provides the necessary tools for professional development. You do not need to worry if you do not have experience with it, it comes with every tool build in it necessary for learning.

  It has its bases on the IntelliJ platform enabling it to provide smart and productive features of code inspection, visual debugging, and also code completion.

- PyCharm Community.
  This is also a free PyCharm edition. PyCharm Community comes along with an intelligent editor, a graphical debugger for your codes, a test runner, tools for inspecting your code, and also for navigation. It is more advanced as compared to the PyCharm Edu. PyCharm Community has, however, fewer features than the PyCharm Professional, as you shall see on the next subtopic.

- PyCharm Professional.
  This is the most advanced edition of PyCharm. PyCharm Professional is paid for, unlike the other editions. It possesses all the features available on the PyCharm Community Edition. Most scientific and web developers utilize in this edition. It offers support for a number of frameworks such as Jupyter, Django, and Flask, and even Database and SQL.
  The extra support that this edition offers that are not available on PyCharm Community includes

scientific tools, tools for website development, Python profiler, and also tools for Database and SQL management.

After installing on the edition of your choice, you can get started with new projects using this text editor. You need to click on "create new project" on your screen, and your new project will pop up.

✓ Eclipse.

To use Eclipse as a Python IDE, you need to install it together with the PyDev plugin. PyDev is a free and open-source plugin that allows programmers to enjoy the features of Eclipse while writing Python lines of code. It has the features of:

- Analyzing and completing code.
- Refactoring.
- Code debugging.
- Providing hints while typing.
- Integration with Django, Jython, Pylint, Unittest and even IronPython.

✓ Gedit.

This is a general-purpose Python text editor for the GNOME environment. It is simple and easy to use as compared to other text editors. You can get started with Gedit on your OS X operating system by going through the following steps:

- Launch on your terminal by hitting on the command button plus the space button. Type the word terminal followed by hitting on the enter button.
- The next step is to install brew on your computing device using some commands from their website.
- The last thing to do is to type in the following command on your terminal
  brew install gedit

The productive features that gedit offers for its users include the following:

- Remote file editing
- File reverting
- Support for print and print preview
- Support for the clipboard commands (cut, copy and paste)
- Wrapping of text
- The numbering of lines

- Highlighting the current line
- Matching of brackets
- Fonts and color configuration
- A complete user manual which is available online
- Backing up of files
- Undo features

✓

TextWrangler

TextWrangler is a free text editor that can be used on any machine using the OS X operating system. It's a mini version of BBedit which has all the required features as BBedit. You can download this text editor online to get started with the TextWrangler text editor.

After installation, go to the right top of your screen, specifically on the search button and type in TextWrangler. You can create your first program by typing in print "My first program". You should then save the file with a .py extension, as it is normally done for all Python files. TextWrangler will display some color effects on your line of code which helps most Python programmers be aware of the syntax errors so as to work on them very easily.

TextWrangler has the following features for its users:

- Navigation of functions
- Feature of coloring the syntax of the lines of code
- Support for opening and saving text files suited on remote FTP servers
- Support for multiple clipboards
- Undo features

✓ Sublime Text

This is a free text editor most users using OS X operating system prefer to use. It offers the best performance since it has a powerful Python API. You can look for a sublime text download setup online and install it on your computing device. Launch the text editor by double-clicking on the file **Sublime Text** which comes with a .dmg extension. You are then required to drag the **Sublime Text 2.app** into the applications folder. Then get rid of the **Sublime Text.dmg** into the thrash. The text editor is then ready for use.

The amazing and beneficial features offered by Sublime Text include the following:

- Users can perform multiple customizations on the editor, unlike other text editors. You can edit on the menus, snippets, and macros.
- It allows users to perform selection on multiple lines of code. This enables faster manipulation of the files.
- It is able to recognize the type of file.
- It highlights the syntax used in the lines of code.
- Automatic indention.
- It offers connectivity with the VSCs (Version Control Systems) such as Git.

Now that you are aware of the different tools of Python development, you can get started with Python on your machine with an OS X operating system.

Python on Windows

Windows operating system does not have a system to support the installation of Python on machines. Therefore, Python is made available to Windows users through the use of MSI packages. These packages have a release for a couple of years that come along with an interpreter and libraries for its users. There are also a number of different installers Windows users can use to get started with Python.

✓ The full installer.
It contains all kinds of components needed by any Python programmer working on any kind of project.

✓ The embeddable package.
This is a minimal Python environment in a zip file that is normally contained in a larger application and thus not directly used by the end-users.

✓ The Microsoft package.
This is the simplest installer Windows users can use when starting off with Python. It provides suitability to execute Python packages and scripts and also provides commands for the Python launching and its tools. It mostly performs better on a Windows 10

operating system. Most students use this package when installing Python on their Windows machines.

This package is free at no cost; you need to select the right package from the Microsoft store. After installing it, you can launch Python from the Windows start button or the command prompt by typing in **Python.**

To make any kind of uninstallation, you can go back to the Windows start button, type in **Python,** right-click on it, and press on uninstall. All packages acquired during installation will be removed but the virtual environments will still remain.

✓ The nugget.org packages.
This is a minimal Python installer on Windows. It promotes the building of the Python packages and scripts execution. Its downside is that you cannot make updates on it and has tools for user interface integrated with it.

Let us now dig deeper into the various steps of getting Python installed on your Windows machine.

✓ Open your browser and go to the official Python website.

✓ Navigate through the download page on the Windows section.

✓ Hit on the link with the latest Python version.

✓ Scroll down the page and click on the setup with the CPU architecture that aligns with your machine which is either 64-bit or 32-bit.

✓ Once the download is complete, double-click on the file.

✓ Then hit on the **install now** section. Your installation is now complete and ready for use.

Python Troubleshooting

Encountering problems with Python on your operating system is a common thing for all beginners in Python. Most of the problems arise due to cramming of syntax leading to errors and bugs. This section will outline some of the common problems and also provide you with different ways of handling them.

✓ Syntax errors.
This type of error can be detected before running on your program. They mostly involve typing errors that do not follow the rules of the Python language, thereby affecting the structure of your lines of code. Syntax errors may arise due to the following reasons:

- Failing to indicate the colons
- Failing to insert brackets
- Misplacing a keyword
- Wrong indentation
- Missing out a keyword

A solution to this problem is to run several lines of code after a while so as you are to rectify the issue as early as possible.

✓ Runtime errors.
These are errors that arise when your program executes. Most of the Python runtime errors are caused by the following:
- Calling on invalid functions
- Using variables on your Python code before defining them
- Failure to indicate quotes on function names
- Dividing variables by zero
- Making access to files or lists which do not exist

✓ Semantic errors.
This is also referred to as the logical type of error. These are errors associated with the design of your lines of code. They do not indicate that you have an error like the above-mentioned errors. They execute

your lines of code incorrectly and give out the wrong output.

They, in short, do not perform their execution as expected. Semantic errors are the toughest type of errors to handle for most of the Python programmers since programmers are forced to go back to their whole lines of code and try to find for the source of error.

Below are some of the causes that lead to the rise of logical errors.

- Writing wrong names for the variables
- Making mistakes on the Boolean values
- Wrong precedence of the operators
- Wrong indentation. Mostly contributed when you copy-paste multiple lines of codes

You should avoid too much copying of the huge blocks of codes.

Chapter 5: List

What is a List?

Python has a total of six sequences built into it with the list being the most common one moreover. This data structure is changeable (mutable). This means that once you create it, you have the ability to change it. Lists in Python are said to be the same as arrays which are used in other various languages such as c++ programming. Having a standardized list format is not always the case, but when studying or actively developing with Python, you find that lists are what you put to use a lot. A list in Python may or may not contain a variety of data types. These data types include integers, strings, and objects. A Python list is helpful when implementing a stack or a queue.

Putting a Python list to use:

- A Python list is a very helpful tool when it comes to protecting your data sequence and iterating the same data sequence.

- A list is executed as a value putting commas to separate between the square bracketing.

- A list in Python is, at all times, ordered and has a given count. The list is indexed starting from zero (0)and the elements follow an indexing scheme depending on the classification.

- A Python list is an example of a container in the structure of data, and they are used to hold numerous amounts of data.

- This Python List stores data elements in a sequential way.

- A Python list is made up of two types of data combination namely heterogeneous or homogeneous.

- A list in Python is the same as the C++ and the C arrays in their respective programming languages.

- When working with many values that are related, a list is the best structure to implement since it enables the collection of data that belong together and keeps it at one reference point. This helps you reduce the size of your code, and the implementation of operation carries the same effect on multiple values at a go.

For the purpose of this beginners guide, let's write a simple list :

#Flying_birds

flying_birds = ['Vulture', 'Swan', 'Crane', 'Goose', 'Mallard', 'Stork']

When we hit the print button, we expect our output to look exactly as the list created:

print(flying_birds)

Output

['Vulture', 'Swan', 'Crane', 'Goose', 'Mallard', 'Stork']

The above elements are in a sequence that is well ordered, and an individual element in the list can be called through indexing.

Indexing of a List

Every item belonging to a list corresponds to an index numerical value, which is an integer starting from 0 as I mentioned above.

For our list flying_birds, the indexing is as follows:

'Vulture'	'Swan'	'Crane'	'Goose'	'Mallard'	'Stork'
0	1	2	3	4	5

From the above items, the first item 'vulture' takes the position of index zero (0), and the list comes to an end at index 5 which is 'stork'.

In Python, each item comes with a specific index number attached to it. This means we can call a specific item individually through its index syntax enabling us to manipulate it as we wish without affecting other items. This is also the same way other sequential data types function.

We can now call an item discretely by referring to its specific index number :

#Flying_birds

Print(flying_birds [2])

Output

Crane

The indexing of the above data is arranged as shown below. You can call a specific item through its index numbers as shown:

Flying_birds[0] = 'Vulture'

Flying_birds[1] = 'Swan'

Flying_birds[2] = 'crane'

Flying_birds[3] = 'Goose'

Flying_birds[4] = 'Mallad'

Flying_birds[5] = 'Stork'

In the event that in flying_birds, we list an index of a number that is more than five(5), the outcome will declare that the item is out of range, and it is not valid.

Print(flying_birds [22])

Output

Index error: the list index is out of range

Apart from applying a positive number index, we are able to get access to items from a list through negative number indexing, but the twist is counting is done backward from the last time in the list, unlike the positive number indexing where counting starts from the first item on the list. In negative indexing, the index number starts at -1. This method of indexing comes in handy when we want to pinpoint a particular item that falls at the end of a given long list.

From our same list on flying_birds, the negative indexing looks like this:

'Vulture'	'Swan'	'Crane'	'Goose'	'Mallard'	'Stork'
-6	-5	-4	-3	-2	-1

Therefore, when you want to print an item by the name 'Mallad' when using the negative index numbering, it should be like this:

Print(flying_bird[-2])

Output

Mallard

Since you have the basic information on how to write a list and how to call a specific item from a list, I will show you how to link a string to a specific item using the plus(+) operator. For this example, our string will be: 'Birds can fly high especially the', and we will use 'Crane' which has an index number of [-4]. Let's do this:

#Flying_birds

Print(' Birds can fly high especially the ' + flying_birds[-4])

Output

Birds can fly high especially the Crane

NB: We were able to concatenate the item at index [-4] with the string ' Birds can fly high especially the '. The plus(+) operator can also be used to link together two or more lists.

How to Change Elements

With Python, you can alter the contents of your list as per your needs.

This is made possible by the indexing of items on a list. By changing the string value of an item at a given index, you can affect what the system prints.

On our list 'flying_birds', we want to change the item at the index position 2 from 'Crane' to 'Alpine Chough'. We do it like this:

#Flying_birds

Flying_birds[2] = 'Alpine Chough'

When we print 'flying_birds', we expect it to read differently:

Print(flying_birds)

Output

['Vulture', 'Swan', 'Alpine Chough', 'Goose', 'Mallard', 'Stork']

This type of change can also be applied to a value in a list by using the negative indexing instead:

Flying_birds[-4] = 'Alpine

Chough' Print(flying_birds)

Output

['Vulture', 'Swan', 'Alpine Chough', 'Goose', 'Mallard', 'Stork']

The results of the negative indexing are the same as those from the positive indexing.

Since this data structure is mutable, it enables us to make changes on a list, especially to a specific part without having to re-write the whole list again, saving us time and allowing updates to be made easily.

How to Remove Element

At this segment, I want to show you how to remove an item from an existing list. Elements in a list are removed using the 'delete' statement. This statement will delete a value at a specified index number.

From our 'flying_birds' list, we want to remove the item 'Goose'. In our list, this item is positioned at index number three(3).To remove this item, we will use the **del** function statement then move on to call the variable list and the index numbering of the item:

#Flying_birds

flying_birds = ['Vulture', 'Swan', 'Alpine Chough', 'Goose', 'Mallard', 'Stork']

del flying_birds[3]

print(flying_birds)

output

['Vulture', 'Swan', 'Alpine Chough', 'Mallard', 'Stork']

After printing the item at index position 3, the string 'Goose' does not appear in our list of flying_birds.

When you have a long list and you want to delete multiple strings, you don't have to delete them at a step-by-step process. You can specify the range and add the delete statement. Say you want to remove not only the item 'Goose' but also 'Mallad' and 'Storks'. We will use the range as shown below :

#Flying_birds

Del flying_birds[3:5]

Print(flying_birds)

Output

['Vulture', 'Swan', 'Alpine Chough']

Apart from the delete statement, you can also use the remove () method to do away with any element in a Python list. The statement functions in a way that when its called, it assumes that the string in the syntax is unwanted and aims to remove it from the list.

In the event that an element is passed to the remove statement and doesn't exist, the system on printing displays a ValueError.

The return() only removes elements from the list; it does not add elements to an existing list.

Example

#Flying_birds List

Flying_birds = ['Vulture', 'Swan', 'Alpine Chough', 'Mallard', 'Stork']

the 'swan' elwment is removed

Flying_birds.remove('swan')

#Update   flying_birds   list

Print('Update list :',flying_birds)

Output

['Vulture', 'Alpine Chough', 'Mallard', 'Stork']

In the event that a list has multiple elements, we can remove them; but the remove element() only removes the first instance example:

#Flying_birds

Flying_birds = ['Vulture', 'Swan', 'Swan', 'Swan' , 'Alpine Chough', 'Mallard', 'Stork']

Remove the swan element

Flying_birds.remove ('swan')

#Update flying_birds list

Print('Update flying_birds list:',flying_birds)

Output

['Vulture', 'Swan', 'Swan' , 'Alpine Chough', 'Mallard', 'Stork']

Here, only the first 'sawn' is removed.

Trying to delete an element that does not exist results in the following error:

Traceback (the last call) :

File "............" line 6 in <module>

Flying_birds.remove ('ostrich')

ValueError: list.remove(6) element at index 6 is not on the list.

This error messaged is displayed because the element Ostrich is not on the list.

Apart from the two methods, you can also use the pop () statement to specifically specify an element that you want to delete.

How to Add Elements

Adding elements in the Python list can be made possible by using append (), insert (), and extend () methods. Let us now get deeper details of the above-mentioned methods.

Append ().

This method is used to add an item at a finishing end of a current list. It does not produce a new list but rather does modification on the already existing list. The syntax normally used for the method is the **list. append (item).** Append () adds items to a list of strings, numbers, and even objects.

Below is a procedure of how to insert an element by applying the method under discussion. There is an example provided below that uses **fruit** as the name of the list.

fruit = ['mango', 'orange', 'banana', 'apple']

This is how you will do it when you want to add another item on the list using append ().

fruit. append ("watermelon")

The **output** will be:

['mango', 'orange', 'banana', 'apple', 'watermelon']

In situations where you want to add another list of objects as a parameter using the append ()

method, this is how you are going to do it.

fruit.append (["pear", "guava", "avocado"])

The **output** will be:

['mango', 'orange', banana', 'apple', 'watermelon', ['pears', 'guavas', 'avocado']]

In a situation where you want to append two arrays using the numpy module, this is how you are going to do it.

In our example, the arrays to be used are:

array1= [2]

array2= [1, 5, 7]

You first need to import the module as **np** then follow the steps below.

array1= np. array([2])

array2= np. array ([1, 5, 7])

result= np. append (array1, array2)

print ('result: ', result)

Output

result: [2, 1, 5, 7]

Extend ().

This method is used to add elements
of one list into another list. Its
syntax is **list.extend (list 1).**
Extend () merges simply merges
two lists. Below is an example
that you can take a keen look at.

list1= ['cookies', 'biscuits',
'juice', 'sweets']

list2= ['cake', 'yogurt', 'soda', 'crisps']

When you want to add the elements
of list2 to list1, this is how you will
do it.

list1.extend (['cake', 'yogurt',
'soda', 'crisps'])

The output will be:

['cookies', 'biscuits', 'juice', 'sweets', 'cake', 'yogurt', 'soda', 'crisps']

Insert ().

This method requires an index and the value to be inserted. Check out the example provided below.

myExample= ['love', 'Python', 'programming']

The element to be inserted at index 0 of the list is I.

These are the detailed steps you need to follow.

myExample.insert (0, "I")

print myExample

Output= ['I', 'love', 'Python', 'programming']

How to Organize a List

Sorting your list when practicing Python can be tough sometimes, right? Do not have any worries because this section is going to guide you on every kind of steps necessary. Python uses the list. sort () method that enables you to organize your list in different ways such as in:

✓ Ascending order.

✓ Descending order.

You can also use a built-in method sorted () that generates a sorted list from any iterable. Most of the Python beginners have issues when deciding on which method to implement during the list organization. You are advised to mostly use the list. sort () method because of various reasons:

✓ List.sort () method is much faster than the other method. It loads the list first followed by the method that calls the function without any arguments as compared to the sorted () method that calls the functions using the list as the arguments.

✓ List.sort () method works with the list in place, and therefore, does not have to make a copy of the list. Contrarily, the sorted () method has to make copies of the list and works with any iterable. This makes a list. sort () method more efficient.

However, both the list. sort () method and sorted () methods organize the lists in ascending by default. This section guides you on the various ways of how to organize your Python lists. It will tackle lists containing numbers, strings, tuples, and also objects.

✓ Numbers.

Sorting numerical in Python is a walk in the park. The list containing numerical in Python is the simple one to organize. Below is an example provided on how to organize your numerical list. **L** will be used to represent the name of the list.

Ascending order

```
L=[67, 3, 16, 74, 2]
L.sort()
print (L)
Output=[2, 3, 16, 67, 74]
```

Descending order.

```
L=[67, 3, 16, 74, 2]
L.sort (reverse=True)
print (L)
```

Output=[74, 67, 16, 3, 2]

If you want to implement on the sorted ()
method, here is how to do it:

Ascending order.
L=[67, 3, 16, 74, 2]
sorted_list= **sorted**
(L) L
[67, 3, 16, 74, 2]
sorted_list
Output= [2, 3, 16, 67, 74]

Sorted () method does not require definition
since it is a built-in function found on
every installed Python.
It does not contain any additional arguments
because it is organizing the values in L
from the smallest to the largest.
This method does not change the
original values of **L** in place.

✓
Strings.
A string is a set of characters. In a scenario
where you are provided with strings and
not numerical, here is a guide on how to
do your organization using both of the
two methods.

Let's say you are provided with a list **F**.

Ascending order

F= ["guava", "mango",
    "pineapple", "avocado"]
F. **sort** ()
F
Output= ['avocado', 'guava',
    'mango', 'pineapple']

Descending order using sorted () method.

F=["guava", "mango",
    "pineapple", "avocado"]
sorted (F, reverse=True)
Output= ['pineapple', 'mango',
    'guava', 'avocado']

In a different scenario where your list of strings is composed of both uppercase and lowercase strings, the output will differ from the rest mentioned above. Uppercase strings in Python are normally treated as lower characters than the lowercase strings. Here is an example that will help you understand better.

Let's say you have a list R, below will be the output.

Ascending order.

R=["town", "country", "Kenya", "home"]

R. **sort** ()

R

Output= ['Kenya', 'country', 'home', 'town']

Case insensitive lists can be sorted through the use of a certain parameter referred to as **key** which is utilized by both the sort and the sorted method. It assists in specifying the function to be called from the items in a list. Take a keen look at the example below.

R=["town", "country", "Kenya", "home"] R. **sort** (key=str.lower) R

Output= ['country', 'home', 'Kenya', 'town']

The str.lower has instructed the sort method to perform the sorting on all the lowercase strings. The parameter has enabled you to define the customized function.

✓ Tuples.

When it comes to tuples, the first element is the one under comparison that makes it similar to how strings are done. Both of the sorting methods can be used when organizing lists in tuples. Take a look at the example given below.

sorted ([(5, 4), (3, 3), (4, 8)])
Output= [(3, 3), (4, 8), (5, 4)]

However, this might not be the case in all situations. Some scenarios might have a tuple whose first element indicates a name while the second element indicates the age of an individual. Such situations will force you to implement the **key** parameter again so as to organize the tuple by age.

You will customize the sorting by defining the key function. You can achieve that by doing the following:

```
#define the custom sort for your list
#return the numerical value of the tuple

L=[ ("Eva", 21), ("John", 53), ("Mary",
    14), ("Reddington", 45) ]
#call on the function
#run the L list
print (L)
#The result will be
[ ('Mary', 14), ('Eva', 21), ('Reddington', 45),
    ('John', 53) ]
```

✓ Objects.

This is the final type of list in Python you are going to learn in this section. In a situation where you are handling objects, you can organize them using the **key** parameter. Let's say you have a **Person** class with attributes of **name** and **age**, this is how you can organize it in Python.

class **Person:**

#Define the variables used

def _init_ (self, name, age)

#Declare the variable name

#Declare the variable age

self. age= age

Try creating objects of the class **Person** and insert them to a list **L**. This is how it can be done.

Mary= Person ('Mary', 14)

John=Person ('John', 53)

Eva= Person ('Eva', 21)

Reddington= Person ('Reddington', 45)

L= [Eva, John, Mary, Reddington]

You can organize the objects of the class by using the attributes that you prefer.

When you make up your mind to use its **name** attribute, this is how it is done.

#assign the key parameter used to a lambda

#run the names of the items in the

list #The result of the code will be:

Output= ['Eva', 'John', 'Mary', 'Reddington']

This is how it is done when you decide to organize the objects by the **age** attribute.

#assign the key parameter to a lambda

#print the names of the elements according to the attribute

#The result of the code will be:

Output= ['Mary', 'Eva', 'Reddington', 'John']

Custom sort definition on any object in Python is a piece of cake. Good luck with that.

Chapter 6:
Variable and
Simple Data
Types

Dictionaries

Dictionaries are data types in the Python programming language that is much similar to a list of certain objects contained in a particular collection. Let us venture into some of the similar characteristics and differences that lists and dictionaries share, so as to get the basic idea of what dictionaries are all about. Similar characteristics of these two data types include: They are both mutable, hence due to any shifting at any particular moment of time, they are dynamic. They are able to change in a way that they are to grow and shrink during any episodes and a dictionary is capable of containing another dictionary in it, and a list is too able to contain another list in it hence concluding that these data types can be nested. The only difference between these two data types comes from how the data values are accessed. Lists are normally accessed by various indexing operations whereas dictionaries are basically accessed by the use of various kinds of keys.

Dictionaries basically consist of some key-value pairs that normally are the key to a specified associated value. We define a dictionary in Python by first enclosing the entire list using curly brackets, placing a full colon that separates the key pairs to the associated value placed, and lastly by using a comma mark in separating the various kinds of key pairs that are available in the dictionary. Another way in which dictionaries can be constructed in the Python world is through the use of dict() function in the program. This one works in a way that the value of the argument in the dict() function consists of the keys and the respective values that have been paired along with it. Kindly remember that square brackets are normally used to contain the key-value pairs in the program in question. Once dictionaries have been defined, it is possible to display its contents where they get displayed just the same way they were defined in a structural manner.

Dictionaries are accessed by specifying its relevant key inside square brackets symbol, and in a case where a certain key does not exist in a particular dictionary, an exception is raised right away as an error made. It is then possible to add a certain entry in a particular dictionary where a new key with its value is assigned in the program. In updating a particular entry, a new value is just assigned to an existing key. During the delete of an entry operation, a del statement is normally used specifying the actual key to delete.

Lastly, methods and various operations are normally implemented in dictionaries so various tasks can be achieved. For example, if a developer has the intention of copying a particular dictionary, he or she is obligated to use the copy() method of the Python programming language.

Some of the other methods include:

- Clear method - this method clears all the kinds of elements that are present in the dictionary.
- Get method - this one gives the value of the key that has been specified in the dictionary.
- From keys - this kind of method gives out a particular amount of keys and values from the dictionary.
- Keys - outputs a list that entails the keys in the dictionary.
- Pop - this method removes the elements with the specified keys.
- Value method – this method gives out a collection of all the values that are present in a certain dictionary.

Functions

A function is defined as a set of various statements that takes in some inputs, computation is then carried out, and output is eventually produced at the end. The purpose of the functions is to evade writing the same set of code all over again during different cases, and instead, just call the function in the program. A function in the Python programming language is created using the def keyword and a certain name which is then followed by the parenthesis and full colon symbols. Calling a function that normally happens at the program consists of the function name that is then followed by the parenthesis symbols. Information is then passed to various functions in the form of parameters that are placed in parenthesis after the function name. Multiple parameters can be placed in the brackets and then separated by the use of commas inside the parenthesis.

In the Python language world, there exist different kinds of parameters that are commonly implemented by a number of Python developers. Default parameters are the kind of parameters that can be defined as a parameter that normally assumes a default value if at all no value has been placed in the function call for that particular argument. There are also keyword arguments which allow a developer to specify a particular argument name with values in a bid for the caller to ignore the order of the parameters in question. To add, there is also the variable-length arguments that normally sums up the normal and keyword variable number of arguments in a particular program that has been coded using the Python programming language.

Looking at the types of functions, there is an anonymous function which is a type of function that does not bear any kind of name and the one that uses the lambda keyword instead.

Classes

A class is basically a code of template that is used in creating various kinds of objects or entirely a major blueprint that is used in creating objects in the Python programming language. Classes consist of member variables with several kinds of methods involved and any other operations that may be involved in the program. A class is constructed by including the keyword class just before the desired class name.

Classes in the Python world normally bear a certain function called init function that normally executes when a particular class is being initiated and where values are being assigned to key-value object properties. This function is usually called automatically every time the class is used to create an object in a particular class. Another term, methods, basically defines the functions that belong to specific objects in the program, and when defining particular methods, you usually provide the first argument to the method using a self keyword. Methods are normally able to access the class attributes in the program.

Testing your Code

In a Python programming language, there are several technique methods that are used in testing a particular kind of code. Let us venture into the actual methods that are normally involved:

- Automated versus manual testing. Exploratory testing is a type of manual testing that is committed without a specific plan, where a developer is just trying to explore the actual application. In a bid to complete certain amounts of manual tests, a developer is obligated to draft a list of all the available features that a certain application contains, the various kinds of inputs that are normally accepted, and the possible expected results. With this, the developer is expected to go back to his or her list whenever changes are made to a particular set of programs, an activity that is so much tiresome and unsatisfying. It is at this point where automated testing comes in.

Automated testing is the execution of the set program of code by a script in place of a particular human. Python language comes in handy is a set of tools and certain libraries that aids a particular developer in making automated testing to its application.

- Unit tests versus integration tests. A unit test is basically a kind of smaller test that checks whether a single component in a particular program works the right way so as to make it functional, whereas an integration test is the type of testing that ensures all the components that are involved in a particular set of program work well with each other. Both unit tests and integration tests can be written in a specific program.

Test runners are basically tools that pick up the source code directory of a particular kind of program that contains unit tests and various settings, gets to execute them, and eventually outputs the results to the log files or the console.

Let us look at some of the common test runners that are used by programmers:

✓

Pytest
This particular test runner supports the execution of various unit cases. Good example of the great characteristics used in pytest test runner include: supports the use of the built-in assert statement instead of using the special self assert method, offers support for filtering various test cases, it has the ability to rerun from the last

test that had failed, and establishes a favorable ecosystem of hundreds of plugins with the intention of extending the functionality.

✓ Unittest.

Unittest is available in the Python standard library since the 2.1 version and can probably be seen in the commercial Python applications and various open-source projects. It contains both a test framework and a test runner. To add, a few requirements are called for when using unittest during testing of your particular program. You are required to put your tests into classes as methods, and one is also expected to use special assertion methods in the particular unittest, for instance, using test case class in place of the built-in the assert statement.

In order for this particular operation to work, one is required to import unittest from the particular standard library, then create a class called test sum that gets to inherit from the test case class, change the test functions into methods by including self as part of the first argument, then change the assertions to use self asset equal method on the particular test case class, and eventually change the entry point of the command line to call unittest main.

✓

Nose or nose2

If you are a novice in using test runners, it is highly recommended that you commence with nose2 in place of the nose when running various kinds of your programs. Nose or nose2 is compatible with multiple unittest frameworks and can be used in place of the unittest test runner for its functions okay. To commence with the nose2 test runner, install the nose2 test runner from pypl and execute it from the command line. The test runner will try to discover all the test scripts named test py and the various test cases that are inherited from the unittest.

File and Exceptions

For file handling operations, Python language treats files as either text or binary, a concept that is so important to most of the programmers and where every line of code that is available composes of a set of characters that eventually form a particular text file. Every line in a file is normally terminated with the presence of special kinds of characters commonly known as the end of line characters like a comma and a new line character. It normally finalizes the current line and then notifies the computer interpreter that a new line has begun. Users are able to handle various kinds of files where they are able to read and write codes, explore the various file handling options as part of the operations that are normally involved in files.

Let us look at some of the operations that are normally involved in the reading and write files:

✓ The open function.

This type of function in the Python programming language normally opens a file in the read and write mode. The open function goes along with just two kinds of arguments, the actual file name and the specific mode, that is whether to read or write. There exist three kinds of modes: reading which is represented by r, w symbol for writing value for appending, and r plus for both reading and writing mode. The mode argument is not usually mandatory, and if not placed in any program, the default mode is normally r for reading mode. Looking at the modes:

- The read mode - in a case where you need to derive a string that entails a string of characters in the file, we utilize the file.read() operation. Alternatively, the programmer can decide to call a specific amount of characters which will then be outputted as a string, and in the exact number that was argument-ed, that is file.read(3) operation.
- The write mode - the file.write() operation is normally used. For instance, file.write("This is the writing program")

that enables you to add up the contents of the particular program.

- The append mode - This one is capable of enhancing clean kind of syntax and exceptions when getting to work with various kinds of codes.

✓

Write a function with the function
> Write function can also be used with function to write some content to a particular set of programs.

✓

Split function.
> Programmers are capable of splitting
> lines using file handling in the Python programming language. This is capable of splitting the variable when any space is encountered, and we may also split any kind of character as per our own desire.

> This and many more other functions are normally involved in file handling operations in the Python programming world.

> Exceptions are the events that normally occur during the

execution of a particular program that disrupts the normal path of various instructions of a particular program. This is basically an object in a Python programming language which normally represents a certain error that has been involved in the program. An exception that has been involved in a program should be handled quickly unless the execution gets to be terminated.

Exceptions can be handled in a way that a programmer can place his or her set of code blocks after a set of the keyword try and a set of full colon symbols prior to it and an except statement after the set of blocks of code. The except statement is then followed by a set of blocks of code that is able to handle the situation in the program the right way.

A few points to take during the above operation are that a single statement can bear several except statements which are super useful when the try block is capable of giving out different kinds of exceptions, a generic except clause can be provided so as to handle various kinds of exceptions. An except clause can also be included where the set of code gets to be executed only when the set of code in the try block does not raise any kind of exception, and the else statement is definitely a good zone for a particular kind of program that does not require any kind of exception to be involved.

Exceptions can also bear arguments that normally give an extra piece of information about a certain problem in question. The contents of the argument vary with each other according to the kind of exception involved, and the variables received can either be single or composed of multiple values that are in the form of tuples. The argument is normally optional; when no argument has been placed in the program, the exception argument becomes none.

Exceptions are raised in various ways using the raise statement as follows: the raise statement, followed by exception, argument, and then the traceback.

The argument at the final and the traceback are usually optional, and if they happen to be present, that becomes the traceback object that gets to be used for the exception. To add, there exist user-defined kind of exception which allow the programmer to create their own exceptions by deriving classes from the standard built-in exceptions that have been used in the program.

User Input and while Loops

A while loop in the Python world is basically used to iterate a particular set of code as long as the specific condition being tested gets to remain true. The body of the program only gets to be executed only if the test condition set gets to remain true and the execution takes place over and over again until the test expression set evaluates to false that will eventually terminate the program. Any non zero that is interpreted is termed as true, whereas the none and zero values are normally interpreted as false.

When while loop with else is used, the else part of the program is normally executed only if the set condition in the while statement is termed to be false. In a case where a break statement gets to be used after the while statement piece of code, the set of code in the else statement gets ignored by the interpreter. Therefore, it can be concluded that when else statement only gets to be executed when the set condition in the while statement is termed to be false and when no break statement has been included after a while set of code statements.

For the user inputs, there are two functions that a programmer can initiate so as to get various kinds of inputs from the user and where the results obtained can be stored into a particular variable in the program.

The raw input function used in the Python programming language is used to read various kinds of strings inputted by the users. For instance, name= raw_input("What is your name?"). On the other hand, the input function can just be able to read integers. For example, age= input("what is your age?")

Exception handling of inputs always ensures that the user has entered some valid kind of information into the program database. One of the ways of ensuring correctness and the accuracy of the information that gets to be inputted by the user is avoiding any kind of errors that may be involved in a particular program. For example, using the while loop command in your particular set of program that has been used which will be executed in a way that the code will continuously run until a valid integer has been inputted by the user in question. Except statements can also be used in the particular program as part of raising an exception, an event that will curb many applications from crashing from time to time, and instead of second printing out of the output gets to be enhanced.

Chapter 7: Data Visualization

How to Generate Data

Data visualization consists of various tools for generating data. The tools used in the generation of visualized data in Python include the following:

✓ Cluvio.
Ever wished for a tool that can enable the creation of exciting visualizations? Cluvio might be the tool that you have been looking for. Cluvio is a company based in Germany that was founded in 2016. It offers exciting and amazing features for its users and enables you to execute SQL queries from your database. More than 100 companies trust this tool of data visualization due to various reasons:

- Amazing usability and design. Cluvio has a great design for its users that is of good quality and a simple interface for the novice Python programmers to understand. The design has high standards that enable the creation of interactive models.

- Supports the analysis of SQL-based data. It analyzes any structured query language data, generates charts, and shares them out which is not seen on other tools for generating data.

- Creates interactive boards. Interactive dashboards are mostly preferred by users. Cluvio generates interactive boards that make data visualization exciting for Python beginners.

- Supports both R language and SQL. Cluvio integrates with both SQL and R languages which makes it a powerful tool. It is able to generate efficient statistical data using the R language that most data engineers use in data visualization. This makes the tool more popular than other tools.

- Suitable for both small and large companies. Cluvio consists of different pricing options that favor both the infant companies and the major companies. It has a free pricing option plan, a starter plan, and also a pro plan for the big companies. Each of the plans has different features for its users.

One of the downsides of Cluvio is that it does not support other file formats such as the CSV and the Excel formats.

✓ Google charts.

You have all heard of Google, right? Google offers vast tools for its users across the world that help in the running and execution of data. A Google chart is one of the tools being offered that assist you in your management and in the presentation of data. Google charts represent and generate your data in the form of piecharts and pictographs. This makes it easier for users to read the data and make the analysis. Google charts are free tools that make them popular as compared to other tools that are offered at a fee.

Moreover, Google charts do not require any programming skills for you to use them. It mostly favors the novice Python programmers who do not have adequate programming skills since they are just starting off their programming journey. They are able to generate visualized data from statistical graphs and piecharts.

Google charts also offer the benefit of free virtualization hosting for its users at no cost. This enables the sharing of data across the website. Google charts also enable programmers to generate on their images from charts and other plots by the use of an API (Application Programming Interface) known as the Image Charts API. With this API, you are only required to establish a URL which will contain your information on the data and its formatting. You do not require any type of coding for you to generate an image from a Google chart.

Its main downside is that it has poor support for its customers, unlike other tools of data visualization. Also, there may be possibilities of the loss of your graphics in situations where the Google servers are down. Many of the novice Python programmers suffer this since they forget to back up their graphics. The final downside of a Google chart is that it denies its users the ability to perform some modifications on their code since the code is not quite exposed.

✓ Infogram.
This is a tool used to generate data from marketing. It has high capabilities for

publishing as compared to the tools mentioned above. Infogram is much popular for its simplicity to use since it contains a user-friendly interface for the novice Python programmers to understand. It also offers great support for customers unlike it is seen on other tools such as the Google charts. Infogram is mostly preferred by the managers and the software engineers involved in the data virtualization.

Infogrames focus on images to be able to generate data. They provide its users with templates that allow customization based on the statistical data and any kind of graphics. It is offered at a fee of approximately $19 per user every month. This makes it unsuitable for not the well-established firms. Its performance is not quite functional as compared to other tools.

✓ Visme.

This is a tool used for the design of shared stories in a way of presentations. Visme consists of three pricing plans which include the individual plan, the business plan, and the education plan. Most individuals utilize this tool due to its simple user interface that provides ease of use. Visme also provides vast graphs and resources that assist in the creation of stable and attractive models. It also offers good quality customer support that helps in assisting the novice Python programmers.

The downside involved for this tool include issues with the text boxes and varying quality of the design when files are exported. This makes it hard for beginners to use. Individuals who mostly prefer this tool are the marketing directors and also the persons involved in media productions.

✓ Flare.

This is an Actionscript library that enables users to create any sort of virtualization from the charts to something interactive. Flare enables you to make presentations of the charts in a reasonable manner. Users also have the capability of making customizations on the dashboards by the use of text boxes so as to point out the insights.

The drawback of this tool is that the virtualization made when using this tool is quite unsuitable for mobile applications. It is also tough to integrate this tool with some website applications. Moreso, the flare tool takes time to be updated and it, therefore, produces outdated dashboards not forgetting the many bugs it contains.

How to Download Data

Gone are the times when most of the novice Python programmers experienced hard times when downloading their visualized data. It has been fortunately made easier nowadays to draw your data by implementing a few modules. The modules being talked about here are Pandas and Matplotlib.

Let us now get into details on the various modules that will help you download your Python data.

✓ Pandas.
They are Python packages with numerous tools for analyzing data. Pandas are used for the management and importation of datasets in Python using a variety of formats. They are also integrated with some of the methods that can assist in the data analysis in Python.

Many individuals prefer using pandas in data visualization due to the following reasons:

- They enable data presentation in a way that can be easily analyzed. They do this via the use of the Series data structure and also DataFrame data structure.
- Pandas consist of a variety of methods suitable for the efficient filtering of data.
- They also contain a set of utilities that support the input and output operations. Pandas can read the different formats of data such as CSV and also ms excel.

How can you install pandas?

Pandas do not come with the normal Python distributions. You need to install them on your terminal to use them. This can be done by the use of the pip command that normally comes with the Python distribution. Run the **pip** command together with pandas on the terminal of your machine.

In situations where you have anaconda already installed on your machine, you can run the **conda** command together with the pandas on your terminal to make the installation successful. You are advised to install the latest version of pandas on your machine. You are now ready to go.

Let us now dig deeper into the two types of data structures mentioned above that are used by pandas in Python.

- Series.
  This type of data structure is the same as a one-dimensional array. A series of data structures provides storage to any type of data, and its values cannot be changed. The first element of the data structure is normally assigned an index value of 0 while the last element is assigned an index of N-1. N represents the total amount of elements in the data structure.

  To first establish the Pandas series:
  ✓ You need to import the pandas' package on your terminal.
  ✓ **Series** is then created by using an array after calling on the **pd. Series ()** method.
  ✓ The contents of the Series will finally be displayed after running on the print () command.

  The output of the content will consist of two columns, whereby the first column will be the indexes of the elements, while the second column will contain the elements used in the array.

A **series** can also be generated by the use of the numpy array then, later on, made some conversion to a Pandas series. This is how it can be done.

#import on pandas on your terminal.

#import on numpy.

#import on the system command.

#call on the file object for the output to be displayed by the print () method.

#call on the numpy library to create an array of your elements

#assign an array to the Pandas series.

#call on the print method to display the output.

The output will contain a first column with the indexes of the elements, and the second column will be elements of your array.

- DataFrame.
  This type of data structure in pandas is in the form of a table that displays data in the terms of rows and columns. It is a 2-dimensional array, unlike what is seen in the Series data structure. The values of

the columns can be modified without affecting their identities.

DataFrame data structures can be generated from scratch, or you can decide to use on the numpy library and convert them later to the data structure.

By building from scratch, you can follow the following steps:

#import pandas on your terminal #create a DataFrame.
#assign DataFrame to a variable using pandas where you also assign the values of the rows and columns as part of your arguments.
#call on the print method to display the output.

The output will also contain a column of indexes at the start just like you have seen on the Series data structure.

How do you retrieve data using pandas?

Pandas can read data from file formats such as CSV, that consist of values separated by commas. This is made possible by the use of the read_csv method.

You need to do the following to achieve the data importation into the pandas DataFrame.

#import on pandas.
#call on the file with the CSV values using the read_csv method. You need to specify the location of the file using arguments.
#call on the print function to display the values of the file.

In situations where you have large datasets, you can retrieve a few numbers of rows you want to retrieve the data from by using the **head ()** method. Moreover, if you want to retrieve a specific row or column of a large dataset, you can use the **loc ()** method.

Pandas can also read and retrieve data from files with the file formats of ms excel with the use of the **read_excel** method.

✓
Matplotlib
Matplotlib is another great visualization library used in Python. It was developed by John Hunter in 2002. It is established on the arrays of NumPy and enables its users to get access to huge amounts of data. Matplotlib is available on Windows,

Linux, and also on OS X operating systems.

This Python library is integrated with the plots of lines, bars, and also histograms that normally assist you in the pattern and trends discovery, and you are also able to make correlations of your data.

Below is the detailed information on the different plots used in Matplotlib.

- Line plot.
  To generate this, you will go through the steps below:
  #import on the Matplotlib Python library.
  #assign values for your x-axis.
  #assign values for your y-axis.
  #plot your values using pyplot function.
  #use the show function to display your plotting.

  Your line plots will finally be generated.

- Bar plot.
  The procedure for this is quite similar to that of a line plot. You

are required to follow the following steps:
 #import on the Matplotlib Python library.
 #assign values for your x-axis.
#assign values for your y-axis.
#plot your bar using the pyplot function.
 #use the show function to display your bar.
Your bar plot will, at last, be displayed by this Python library.

- Histogram.
  On this plot, you are required to call on the import function of Matplotlib, and then assign values for both the y-axis and the x-axis. Make plotting of your histogram using the pyplot function and then call on the show function to display the histogram.

How to Work with APIs

An Application Programming Interface (API) is a software that acts as an intermediary between two applications and enables them to work together. Let us apply a real-life example for you to understand better. In a situation where you are a customer in a certain restaurant, you need to make an order to the waiter for you to get served with a meal of your choice. Therefore, you will make an alert to the waiter who will take your order to the kitchen team since they have the responsibility of preparing your meal. The meal gets prepared, and the waiter will bring the meal back to you. The waiter in our case scenario is the API while you, as the customer, are the system user, and the kitchen team act as the system you are using. The point is now at home, right?

This section is going to cover the different ways of working with APIs used in data visualization. Some of the APIs used in data visualization include the following:

✓ Bokeh.
This API was established by a development team of Anaconda back in 2012. It is a free API with no cost and was created to visualize the data applications from web browsers. Most individuals prefer using this API because it enables them to establish on their statistical plots, and it also supports data visualization from other Python libraries such as Matplotlib.

Bokeh has three types of levels for different persons who have varying levels of control. The uppermost interface of this

API is designed for the creation of simple charts using different methods of histograms, line plots, and also the bar plots. You can acquire the plots by implementing on the numpy arrays and also the DataFrames.

The interface at the middle level enables you to have control of the blocks building the charts. The lowest level is specifically designed for the developers and engineers of software. They normally study every data element of the charts.

✓ Seaborn.
This is a top-level interface that has its bases on the Matplotlib Python library. It promotes the creation of exciting and attractive plots. It is more powerful than the Matplotlib since it can generate a graph with only one line of code unlike when you are using Matplotlib.

Seaborn can be integrated with the DataFrames of pandas, and therefore, be able to produce amazing interfaces. The downside of this API is that you need to be aware of how Matplotlib works to have an easy time when working on the Seaborn API.

✓ Plotly.

Plotly is a stable data visualization API mostly for websites. Are you aware that this API can be accessed from a Python notebook which makes it unique from the rest of the API? It is considered as a special API since it possesses the functionality of 3D charts. Plotly supports many file formats such as CSV and the xls formats. It enables its users to simply make modifications on the graphs. Also, Plotly has great compatibility with many languages such as R and Python and tools like Matlab.

✓ Pygal.

Pygal is quite similar to Plotly and Bokeh. It is mostly used for Python data visualization, but it is also considered to be used in HTML projects. It provides plots with interactions that are normally on the online web browsers. Pygals produce plots as Scalable Vector Graphics (SVG) that are not found on any other data visualization APIs.

It is, however, suitable for small datasets. In situations where you use large datasets, the charts become slow, and they become difficult to process the data.

Pygal also enables the creation of amazing and attractive charts with the use of a few lines of code.

✓

Geoplotlib.
Geoplotlib is an API that is mostly concerned with the geographical location and is also involved in the generation of maps. The kind of maps that can be generated when you use this API is the chloropleths and also the dot density maps. You need to install Pyglet on your machine when you decide to utilize Geoplotlib.

This API comes in handy when you do not have adequate tools for maps since most of the standard Python installation does not have tools for maps.

✓

Gleam.
This is another amazing data visualization API. It can integrate with any Python library. It provides its users with the ability to switch any analysis to an interactive website application with the use of any scripts of Python programming. You do not require to have any skills of HTML, CSS, and JavaScript to use this API. This is the reason why most individuals prefer using it.

✓ Altair.

This is a simple Python library used in statistics and is established on the Vega and the Vega-Lite. Many individuals prefer it because it is user-friendly that makes them be able to understand well. Its source can be obtained from Github. It supports the creation of attractive data visualizations with only a few lines of code unlike it is seen on other data visualization APIs.

Altair performs better on a Jupyter notebook, and it can be installed on your computer using the **conda** command. The steps involved to create a simple Altair chart include the following:

- Generate an object for the chart using a DataFrame for Pandas.
- Select the right marking for your chart.
- Assign values to the x-axis and the y-axis using the **encode** command with the right number of columns.

✓ ggplot.

This is a Python library mostly based on ggplot2 which is an R system. ggplot enables you to come up with plots containing a peak level of grammar. It has tight integration with pandas. Its user interface is simple and exciting to learn from as compared to other APIs which are complex that turn off most novice Python programmers. The charts on ggplot are easy to customize, and they offer elaborate views for you to easily understand. Ggplot also merges multiple datasets into one graph.

ggplot has its downsides that include:
- Requires more lines of code, unlike other APIs.
- Its production results might be at fault since it mainly focuses on establishing attractive graphs with amazing color schemes.

Chapter 8: Web Applications

A web application runs on a remote server as a software application. Most the time, web browsers are for web applications like the internet. Some of the applications are used for intranets, schools, firms, and organizations. They are not the same as other applications since you do not need to install them. Some of the common web applications include Flickr, Wikipedia, Facebook, and Mibbit. They are popular since most of the operating systems are on the web browser and programmers can change them with ease.

Several benefits come with using web application:

- They do not need to be installed since they run inside a browser.
- They do not require a lot of space for storage only a display of data.
- With web applications. It helps with compatibility problems; all is needed is a browser.
- Most of the data used are remotely stored; hence ease of cooperation and communication.

- Web application helps in mail and communication.

Apart from the listed benefits of web applications, there are also drawbacks:

- Most of the known web applications will seem to look different as compared to the regular programs. The reason is that they run inside a browser. The user experience might be different and not liked by many.
- To be able to follow standards, web applications need to be coded, and any small changes will prevent the web application to be used in any browser.
- There is a need to have a connection between the web application and the server in order for it to run smoothly. For the connection to happen, you will need bandwidth. And when the connection is not adequate, you may experience data loss or the application will be usable.
- Most of the web applications depend on the server that hosts them. When it is off, the web application is not usable, but the traditional applications will still work.
- The overall control of the web application is with the mother company. They have the power to create a new version when they feel like it.

- When the data is remotely stored, exporting it to be used by other applications will be hard.
- Web applications enable the company to track all the activities of the users, hence privacy issues.

At this point, you need to know how a web application works. Most of the web applications are coded in a language that is browser supported, like HTML or JavaScript. And the main reason is that the languages depend on the browser in order to execute their programs. You should know that some of these applications are dynamic, and they will require server-side processing. Others are considered static and will not need any processing from the server.

When you have a web application, you will need a webserver to manage all the requests that the client has. The server will help in performing all the tasks and store data and information. The application server includes ASP, PHP, and JSP. A normal web application has a specific flow:

- The user will trigger a request using the internet that goes to the webserver. This can be done through the web browser or user interface on the application.
- The web server will then forward that request to the specific web application server.

- The requested task will be performed by the web application server; this includes querying the database or data processing that will generate the required results.
- The results will be sent to the web server by the web application server; this is in regards to the data processed or the required information.
- The client will get a response from the webserver; they will get the information that they have requested and it will appear on the user's display.

There are several examples of web applications such as shopping carts, word processors, online forms, file conversions, and scanning, online forms, and email programs like Yahoo and Gmail.

How to Work with Django

Django is used to create web applications. It is specifically meant to create a web application that connects to a database. You can also deal with user management, good security, and internationalization. Some of the common web applications include Disqus, Pinterest, and Instagram. You can use Django as standalone libraries even though it will require extra work. That is the reason why it is not advisable to use it as a standalone.

Django is a combination of different components that work by responding to user requests.

- The first step is the request-or-response system. The main work is to receive and return web responses. Django will accept all the requests of the URLs and return all the HTML information to the web browser. The page can be in plain text or something better.

- The web requests will enter the Django application through the URLs. The only entry point for any Django application is the URLs; developers have the control of the available URLs. When you access the URL, Django will enable the viewing.

- All your requests will be processed by the views. Django views are considered to be codes generated from Python when the URL is accessed. Views are something simple like returning a text to the user. The text can be made complex. It can be form processing, credit card processing, and database querying. When the view has completed processing, a web response is sent to the user.

- When web response is returned, the user can access the URL on the browser they will access the response. This could be an HTML web page that shows a combination of images and text, and they are created using the templating system from Django.

- With Django information, there is flexibility to have more applications. You can use that you create a simple blog, mobile applications, or a desktop. Django framework is powered by sites like Instagram and Pinterest.

User Accounts

A user account is on the network server that is used to store the username of the computer, password, and any relevant information. When you have the user account, it will allow you or not to connect with other computers or networks. With a network with multiple users, you will need user accounts. A good example of a user account is your email account.

There are different types of user accounts, regardless of the operating system that you are using. You will be able to trace, authenticate, and monitor all the services. When you install an operating system, it creates user accounts to have access after the installation. After the installation, you will have four user accounts; system account, super user account, regular and guest user account.

- **System account**: These are accounts that are used to access resources in the system. The operating system will use these accounts to know if a service is allowed to access the resources or not. When they are installed, they create relevant accounts; and after installation, the account will be able to access the needed information. If you are a network or system administrator, you will not need to have any information about the accounts.

- **Super user account**: This account is privileged in the operating system. When one is using Windows, the account is referred to as the Administrator account. When using Linux, the account is the root account, and the operating system will help the user complete different tasks. Tasks are like starting services, creating and deleting new user accounts, installing new software, and changing system files.

- **Regular user account**: This account does not have many privileges and cannot make changes in the system properties and files. They only operate on tasks that they are authorized like running applications, creating files, and customizing variables.

- **The Guest user account**: This is the account that has less privilege; you will not be able to change anything with the system. The account is known to perform temporary tasks like playing games, watching movies, or browsing the internet. Using Windows, this account will be created after installation; and in Linux, you will need to create the account manually after installation.

The next step is to know how to create a user account. When you have multiple users using the same computer, you will need to have new user accounts for each user. When using Windows, you can create several accounts. Each of the user accounts has its own settings. It will allow you to control the files separately, and when each user logs in, it will be like their own computer.

The first step in creating a user account is to click on START on the CONTROL PANEL then click on ADD or REMOVE user accounts. Click on CREATE A NEW ACCOUNT and choose the account type. You will enter the account name and then select the account type that you wish to create. The administrator has the privilege to create and change accounts and installing programs. The difference is a standard user cannot perform such tasks. The last step will be to click on the CREATE ACCOUNT button and close the CONTROL PANEL.

How to Style and Deploy an App

There are different deployment options that need to be considered. When an app is developed in the application builder, it is created in the workplace. All the workplaces have IDs and names; all you need is to create an application in the development and then deploy it in production.

During deployment, you will decide where you want the existing ID to be in the workplace, existing HTTP server, or in creating new ones. The deployment options include:

- You will first create an application that is expressed by end-users. The best way to deploy an application is by creating an Application Express for end users. Then sent the URL and login details to the users. It will work when the user population is tolerant and small.
- You will need to use the same schema and workplace. You need to export and then import the application, then install that under a different application ID. This strategy will work when there are fewer changes to any known objects.
- Use the same schema and a different workplace, export all, and then import the applications into another workplace. It

will prevent any production and modification by developers.

- Use a different schema and workspace. Export and then import the application into a separate workplace, and install it in a separate schema.
- Use a different database for all variations. Export then import to another oracle application and then install it to a different database and schema.

To deploy an app, in the configuration manager console, click on SOFTWARE LIBRARY. Go to APPLICATION MANAGEMENT and then choose APPLICATION or APPLICATION GROUP.

Choose from an application or application group from the deploy list and click DEPLOY.

Conclusion

Thanks for making it through to the end of Python Crash Course: *A Complete Step-by-Step Beginner Guide for Python Coding, NumPy, Pandas, and Data Visualization*. This book is meant for beginners, experts, and professionals who are interested in Python programming. This book will highlight all that is needed in Python programming, what Python programming is and its uses.

At this point, you clearly understand who can use Python and its importance to any economists and finance experts. The information will help to know how you can earn as a Python programmer, the basic concepts, and all the terms used in Python programming. You can now start your Python programming for data analysis, how to install Python, and the different places you can learn all this.

With an interactive and educative book, it is easy to understand the operating systems that are used in Python programming. About Linux, OS X, and Windows, you are able to do all the troubleshooting. You know the cost required for Python programming, the courses to learn, and the job you will get after learning. Do you know what a list is? If not, do not worry.

The book will explain all that, how to change, remove, and add the elements. There are data types and visualization. It's about how to generate, download data, and how to work with APIs. The web application is another chapter that is explained, how to work with Django, different user accounts, and how to deploy an app.

We thank you again for choosing to download this book. We believe you did find the book educative and engaging. A positive review on Amazon will be appreciated.